6014 -

W9-AVK-105

YOU CHOOSE
BOOKS

CAN YOU SURVIVE AN

ALIEN INVASION?

An Interactive Doomsday Adventure

by BLAKE HOENA
illustrated by PAUL FISHER JOHNSON

CAPSTONE PRESS
a capstone imprint

You Choose Books are published by Capstone Press,
1710 Roe Crest Drive, North Mankato, Minnesota 56003
www.capstonepub.com

Library of Congress Cataloging-in-Publication Data
Hoena, B. A., author.
  Can you survive an alien invasion? : an interactive doomsday adventure /
by Blake Hoena.
      pages cm.—(You choose books. you choose : doomsday)
  Summary: "A You Choose adventure about surviving an alien invasion"—Provided
by publisher.
  Audience: Ages 8-12
  Audience: Grades 4 to 6
  Includes bibliographical references and index.
  ISBN 978-1-4914-5853-2 (library binding)
  ISBN 978-1-4914-5926-3 (paperback)
  ISBN 978-1-4914-5938-6 (ebook pdf)
1. Human-alien encounters—Juvenile literature. 2. Disasters—Juvenile literature.
3. Survival—Juvenile literature. 4. Plot-your-own stories. I. Title.
  BF2050.H63 2016
  001.942—dc23   2015002015

Editorial Credits
Anthony Wacholtz, editor; Bobbie Nuytten, designer;
Wanda Winch, media researcher; Kathy McColley,
production specialist; Nathan Gassman, creative director

Photo Credits
Shutterstock: CS Stock, (background, throughout), Nevada31, 106, Stefano Garau,
100, Stocksnapper, 103, Ursatii, 104

Printed in Canada.
032015   008825FRF15

TABLE OF CONTENTS

ABOUT YOUR
ADVENTURE

YOU are living through a dark and dangerous time in the near future of humanity. An advanced alien race has invaded Earth, their purpose yet unknown. How will you survive? Start off by turning the page, then follow the directions at the bottom of each page. The choices you make will change your outcome. After you finish your path, go back and read the others to see how other choices would have changed your fate. Do you have what it takes to survive doomsday?

YOU CHOOSE the path you take through an Alien Invasion.

ALIEN INVASION!

The distant city is surrounded in a hazy glow. With all its neon signs and street lamps, the stars are barely visible from the rooftop of your apartment building. That's why you're standing out in the middle of a field on a school night—to get a clear view of the sky. Thousands of brilliant points of light dot the darkness above.

Your best friend, Jacob, was supposed to be here with you. You are working on an astronomy project together. He said he'd meet you just after sunset, but that was an hour ago.

You glance at your phone. He hasn't returned any of your texts. Worry fills your thoughts. *Did his parents ground him? Did he crash his bike?*

You can't let Jacob's tardiness stop you. Your curfew is in a couple of hours, and you need to make some observations to complete your assignment.

Turn the page

You just wish Jacob was here to help. You had to lug your gear all the way from the side of the road, where you left your bike, to a clearing in the field. That was after the 5-mile bike ride to get here, which wasn't easy with your telescope strapped to your back. But at least everything is set up now.

Your telescope has an 80mm refractor lens, and on a clear night, you can see the rings of Saturn. Tonight, you're actually hoping to chart a couple of Saturn's larger moons. That should earn you an A on your project.

You check your phone again. Nothing.

Where is Jacob?

You will have to start without him. You turn to your telescope and spot Saturn low in the sky. It's a bright unblinking dot amongst the dimmer, twinkling stars. You aim your telescope in its direction and bend over to peek through the eyepiece.

After fiddling with the controls for a moment, you bring the planet into focus. Saturn's rings have a 3D effect, making the planet look like it's just hanging there in front of you.

Suddenly, a flash of light fills the lens and blinds you. You stagger backward.

What was that? you wonder, as you rub the fuzziness from your eyes. *A meteor?*

But once your vision clears, you are amazed at how wrong you are. Hovering high up in the sky is a large bluish light surrounded by several smaller swirling lights. They are all too big to be planets or stars and moving around too randomly to be satellites. One swoops down near the ground and then shoots back up to rejoin the others. Another darts ahead of the rest, only to regroup a second later.

Your imagination can come up with only one answer to what they might be. It's a thought that both frightens and excites you: *UFOs!*

Turn the page

That has to be it. Nothing else could move like they do. Not weather balloons or airplanes, birds or bugs.

Your heart begins to race. If only Jacob were here, you'd have someone to back up your story. No one's going to believe you saw a UFO.

You start to turn your telescope toward the alien craft to get a better look at them, but they quickly scatter. Only the largest of the lights holds its place in the sky. You wonder if it's the mother ship.

One of the smaller lights settles behind some trees along the edge of the field. Having an alien spaceship land so close frightens you. It could be dangerous, yet curiosity is urging you to investigate.

To investigate the UFO, turn to page 12.
To get away from the UFO, turn to page 16.

This is an opportunity you can't pass up. You have to see what the aliens look like. And you have to take a few photos—proof for those people who won't believe you actually saw a UFO.

You grab the pack lying next to your telescope. Inside is a flashlight with red film taped over the end of the lens. You flick it on, and it glows red. It's a trick you learned in your astronomy class. Red light does not affect your night vision.

The alien ship is in the opposite direction of your bike, but you don't care, even if it means staying out past curfew and possibly getting in trouble. Your parents will understand when they see the pictures.

You jog across the field, keeping your flashlight aimed low at the ground so you can avoid any ruts in the field. You have to slow down when you get to the trees. Branches swat at your face and arms. Roots threaten to trip up your feet.

You creep through the brush as quietly as you can. When you near the edge of the foliage, you stop and duck behind a tree. Peeking around its trunk, you spot a disc-shaped craft in a clearing. It hovers a few feet above the ground. A sphere of blue light protrudes from the bottom and crackles with the hum of energy. The ship is small. It can't be more than 20 feet in diameter and is probably six feet high.

Might be a scout ship, you think.

Turn the page

You want to sneak closer to get a better look. But then a hatch opens in the bottom of the craft. You duck back behind the tree.

What descends from the opening isn't a little green man—it's a robot. The robot stands about waist high and is shaped like a large soda can. It hovers inches above the ground on a smaller version of the blue energy orb that powers the spacecraft.

Numerous antennas stick out from the robot's body. They whirl and jerk about as they scan the area. Several arms with clawed hands extend from panels on the robot. The hands reach down to pick up rocks, leaves, twigs—anything they can find. The items are then deposited in an opening atop the robot. It looks like it's gathering samples, but why?

To take a picture of the UFO, turn to page 18.
To try to make contact with the aliens, turn to page 21.

You've never really believed in aliens. Until now. That was mostly because the people who tell stories about them always seemed a bit odd. But now that you've seen a UFO, you don't want to risk being poked and prodded by little green men. So you pack up your telescope and gear. You sling the bag over your shoulder. Then you hunch down, and as quickly as you can, you jog toward your bike.

Despite the possible danger, you regret not getting any pictures. It would be cool to have proof that you saw a UFO. You're pretty sure if you mention anything to your friends, they'll call you nuts and tease you about it.

You glance back, curious to see where the alien ship is. To your surprise, it's now hovering over the clearing where you had set up your telescope. A green beam of light shines down from the ship. The light whirls around on the ground as if scanning for something.

Do they know I'm out here? you wonder.

Then the green light stops on something for just a moment before it starts combing over the ground you had just crossed. The ship slowly moves in your direction. You start to worry that the aliens know you're out, and you wonder about their intent. Are they friendly or not?

You've read plenty of stories about alien encounters. Some people black out. They may wake hours or even days later not realizing any time has passed. Many of them can't recall what happened to them. You instinctively look down at your phone, to check the day and time, just in case. Then you turn to run.

In the distance, you see a pair of headlights cutting through the night. A car speeds down the road toward you.

To run for your bike, turn to page 23.
To try to stop the car, turn to page 24.

As you lean around the tree, you pull your phone from your back pocket. The spaceship looms over the clearing. There are no windows or visible hatches on its surface, except the opening through which the robot descended. You can't tell if anyone is looking back at you, or even if there are aliens flying the ship.

The robot continues to gather samples. As it nears your hiding spot, you focus the phone's camera on it. You hear a soft click, and there's a bright flash as your phone snaps a picture.

The robot immediately stops. All of its antennas click and whirl in your direction.

Uh-oh!

From the bottom of the UFO, a green light beams down on the ground. The beam whips back and forth across the clearing as if it's searching for something. Any plants caught in the light begin to shrivel and wilt. You watch in horror as the beam makes its way toward you.

Turn the page

Another robot descends from the opening in the spaceship. This one looks different than the first. More menacing. It's almost bullet-shaped, with a red glowing light on top. It immediately begins to follow the green beam of light, which is closing in on you.

You worry that you will be spotted if you move from behind the tree. But as the beam nears your hiding spot, a wave of nausea washes over you. You feel like throwing up or passing out. All around you, leaves brown and shrivel.

Then the robot reaches the edge of the clearing. From a panel in its side, an arm extends with a whirling blade. It starts buzzing through the foliage.

Fear grips you, and you turn to flee.

A beam of red light erupts from behind you. You feel the heat of the blast as it barely misses you, scorching the ground ahead.

You run for your life.

Turn to page 27.

You've read all the weird and frightening stories about alien abductions—none of which you believe. The people behind those stories always seemed a bit odd. You'd probably be the first normal person to see and meet an alien. People would believe you. You're sure of it.

Unless meeting the aliens is what messed up those other people, you wonder.

Still, you want to have solid proof of this meeting, so you pull out your phone. You bring up a video app and start recording as you step from your hiding spot.

You are watching the screen of your phone and not where you are walking. As you enter the clearing, a twig snaps underfoot. Suddenly, all of the robot's antennas snap in your direction. It beeps and buzzes at you as its arms retract into their panels.

Turn the page

"Um, hi," you say nervously, not knowing whether the robot will actually understand you. "I won't hurt you."

The alien robot doesn't move, so you take another step forward. Then another. You cautiously approach as the robot continues to click and beep at you. Not wanting to miss anything, you continue to record what's happening.

You are close enough to reach out and touch the robot when a green beam of light shoots down from the bottom of the UFO behind it. The light quickly whirls around on the ground. You watch in amazement as plants shrivel up in its wake. Then the light washes over you. Nausea grips your stomach. As you double over, your legs give out. You drop your phone and collapse to the ground. The last thing you remember is rising up from the ground and floating toward an opening in the bottom of the ship.

Turn to page 30.

In the stories you've read about alien encounters, cars stall and lose power. You let your telescope slide from your shoulder, knowing you'll be faster without it. You take off for your bike, which is hidden behind a bush along the side of the road.

Meanwhile, the alien craft veers toward the approaching car. The vehicle's lights flicker, and the car stalls in the middle of the road. The UFO's green light washes over the car. The passenger door opens, and an unconscious woman collapses to the ground.

Then a panel opens in the bottom of the spaceship. As if by magic, the woman is lifted off the ground. She begins to float toward the opening of the ship. While you would like to see what happens next, this is your chance to get away.

Realizing you'd be easily seen on the road, you ditch your bike and head out on foot instead. There is a grove of trees about 50 yards from you. You run for cover as fast as your legs will carry you.

Turn to page 27.

You want to get away, and in a hurry. So you dart into the middle of the road and wave your arms frantically. The approaching car's headlights blind you, and for a second, you aren't sure the car is going to stop.

A horn blares. Tires screech. You squint your eyes shut. Then silence. The car has skidded to a halt just feet in front of you.

You run to the passenger side of the car. A young woman rolls down the window.

"Is something wrong?" she asks.

The man driving yells, "You nearly got yourself killed!"

You point at the approaching alien ship.

"Is that a …" the woman's voice trails off as she goes pale.

"Get in!" the man shouts. You immediately jump into the back seat.

Turn the page

As the UFO gets closer, the car's tires squeal. You race forward with the UFO in pursuit. You look out the rearview window, watching in horror as the alien ship easily catches up to you. It positions itself directly over the car. The headlights flicker. The engine sputters and stalls.

"Derek, do something!" the young woman shouts.

The driver hopelessly cranks on the ignition. "It won't start!"

We gotta run, you think. But before you can get the words out, the green light shines down on the car. A wave of nausea washes over you.

"I'm gonna be sick," the man says as he opens his car door.

You open your door as well, but your legs won't work. You fall out, unconscious.

Turn to page 30.

You ruth through the trees as branches swat at your face and scratch your arms. Your side hurts, and your lungs burn as you suck in air. But fear propels you forward. What you saw back there scared you more than you've ever been scared before. And no matter what, you know that you don't want to be caught under the alien ship's green light. Who knows what will happen to you then.

You're not sure how long you've been running. You glance back to see if you're being followed. The UFO isn't in sight. Everything is dark behind you.

Maybe it's safe, you think. *At least for now.*

You slow your pace to a fast walk so that you can catch your breath. You pull your phone out of your back pocket. You have to tell someone what has just happened.

Turn the page

Wow! There's like a hundred texts from Jacob.

You start to read them:

Dude, you there?

You won't believe what I just saw. A UFO!

Seriously. I'm not crazy.

That's why he was late. Maybe he saw the same alien ships that you saw.

You start shooting back replies:

I know. I saw them too.

Stay away from the green light!

You stop for a moment to wait for a response.

None.

Then you notice that Jacob's last text was sent about an hour ago. That's before you even saw the aliens.

Did they get him? You worry.

As you continue to scroll through the rest of his texts, your screen goes blank.

What happened? you wonder. *Did I lose reception?*

You push the message button several times. Nothing pops up. You hold your phone up in the air, but that doesn't help either. As you glance up, you see hundreds of flares exploding high above you. It's like a fireworks display across the whole night sky.

Satellites? That's when you realize what's happening: *The aliens are destroying Earth's communication satellites. That's why my phone went dead.*

As if on cue, you see a green light flash behind you. The alien ship is flying just above the trees and speeding in your direction. You need to find a place to hide. Somewhere that will protect you from the UFO's green light.

Near you is a thick clump of brush. Farther ahead, you see a farmhouse with some lights on.

To hide in the brush, turn to page 33.
To run for the farmhouse, turn to page 38.

When you wake, a bright light shines down, blinding you. You turn away, finding yourself face to face with a robot. Only, it doesn't have a face—just many arms. Some end in needles and scalpels. Others end in antennas and things with functions you can't even imagine.

You try to kick your legs, but they are strapped down. You want to push the robot away, but your arms are bound. So you do the only thing you can do—you scream at the top of your lungs.

"HELP! HELP! HELP!"

The robot doesn't even flinch. It keeps going about its business, probably knowing that there is no one who will hear you.

From a panel in the robots side, an arm pops out with a light at the end of it. The arm starts to whirl about, and light forms a circle in front of you.

Turn the page

Then the robot buzzes three times. You stop your screaming to listen.

Maybe it's trying to communicate, you think.

There's a pause before the robot emits another buzz. Then four quick buzzes. And then one more buzz before it pauses again.

But this time, the robot waits for a few moments, as if it's expecting a response. All the while, its spinning arm continues to circle around and around, creating a perfect ring of light above you. You think the robot is watching you as its antennas click and whirl in your direction.

Then the robot repeats the pattern. Three buzzes. Pause. One buzz. Four buzzes. One buzz.

What does it mean? you wonder. *Is it a code, like Morse code?*

If you know what the buzzes mean, turn to page 35.
If you don't know what they mean, turn to page 65.

You've seen how fast the alien ships can fly. You've watched them dart across the sky. So you worry that the farmhouse is too far away. You might not make it in time, and there's a chance you couldn't even get in if you did make it. Your only hope is to hide.

You duck into the brush, suffering several cuts and scrapes as you burrow deep into the foliage. Once leaves and branches block out the night sky, you stop and wait.

The ship hums loudly as it nears you. Green light fills the area and even reaches you in your hiding spot. You start to feel sick as you watch the leaves shrivel around you. You feel like throwing up and passing out all at the same time, and you curl up into a ball in your hiding spot.

Then a moment later, you hear the buzz of the ship zipping by. You wait a bit longer before daring to crawl out of the brush.

Turn the page

As you untangle yourself from the shrub, you spot a robot approaching. It is bullet-shaped with a glowing red light on top. The robot hovers a few inches above the ground on a blue ball of energy similar to what the UFO uses. It stands about waist high and has several antennas sticking out of side panels. They whirl about, scanning the area.

You think of ducking back into the brush, but the robot's antennas twitch in your direction. You've been spotted.

Then the top of the robot begins to glow bright red. You turn to run, but it's too late. A red burst lights up the night, and you collapse to the ground, dead.

THE END

To follow another path, turn to page 10.
To learn more about aliens, turn to page 101.

"3.141," you whisper. "That's the first four digits of Pi." That's what the buzzes represent. And the circle of light—you need Pi to figure out the area or circumference of a circle.

Your recognition prompts a series of clicks and ticks from the robot. Its arm stops spinning the light and retracts into the side panel. Then you watch helplessly as other arms connect a wire to your forehead.

Your mind is instantly flooded with images. First a distant view of a green and blue Earth. Then fighter jets being zapped out of the air by alien spacecraft. Tanks exploding. A green light washing over soldiers, who instantly collapse.

You realize you're seeing visions of the fighting that's happening all over the world. It is an invasion, and the aliens are trying to show you how badly the war is going for humans.

Turn the page

Then the images turn less deadly, but are equally as destructive. They show huge spacecraft flying over swaths of forests. The ships harvest everything in their paths: plants, trees, animals. They leave behind barren earth.

They're after food. That's why the aliens have invaded.

The last images are of alien ships leaving behind a less green world, but at least leaving the planet intact. The message is clear, and now you know the aliens' purpose.

The robot starts to unstrap your restraints. Behind it, a door slides open.

To try to escape, turn to page 42.
To go peacefully, turn to page 44.

There are lights on in the farmhouse, so you hope there are people home. Maybe they know what's going on. At the very least, maybe they can help you hide.

You sprint to the front door and give it several loud raps. A second later, the door creaks open just enough for a pair of eyes to look out. It's a girl about your age.

"Wh-who is it?" You can tell she's terrified.

"Quick, let me in, " you shout. "There are aliens after me!"

"So what they're saying on TV is real?" she asks. "Not like that H.G. Wells thing?"

"They're real," you reply. "And they're here."

The girl's eyes go wide. You turn around and see the alien ship fast approaching.

"Quick," she says. "Get inside."

She lets you in, then slams the door shut, locking it. Just inside stand two young boys. They stare at you wide-eyed. Behind them is a static-filled TV screen.

"I'm babysitting, and I'm responsible for these boys," she says nervously. "What should we do?"

"Is there somewhere to hide?" you ask. "A basement?"

She nods. Grabbing the boys by their arms, she leads you to a door, which opens up to a set of stairs.

"It's a storage cellar."

She's about to flick on the light when you stop her.

"They might see us," you say.

In the dark, you creep down the stairs behind the girl and boys. There are a couple narrow windows, and you see the ground outside is awash in green light. The edge of the ship hovers over the house.

Turn the page

"Over here," the girl whispers.

There are several shelves full of camping gear. You see sleeping bags and a hatchet, plus pots, coolers, and fishing poles.

"I'm gonna throw up," one of the boys says.

You can feel it too. The green light from the alien ship is getting stronger. Being in the basement of the house isn't shielding you from its effect.

"They must be just outside the house," you say.

"Do you think they'll try to get in?" the girl asks.

To hide in the camping gear, turn to page 48.
To defend yourself against the aliens, turn to page 49.

As soon as you're free from your restraints, you kick at the robot, knocking it backward. Its antennas whirl and buzz as the robot beeps and buzzes loudly. Claw hands shoot from panels on its side. They reach and snap for you, but you're too quick. In an instant, you're on your feet and running.

You dart out the door, but you don't know where to go. You just hope that at some point you find a way out. The ship didn't seem that big when you first saw it, so an exit has to be near. But then a scary thought crosses your mind, *What if I'm not in one of the smaller ships, but the mother ship?*

You don't let that thought stop you. The hallways are narrow and low. You have to hunch over to get through them. Maybe the aliens really *are* little green men. But then you think back to the short robot in the exam room, and you understand that these passageways are designed for robots.

Are there actually any aliens? you wonder. So far you've only seen robots. But right now, that's the least of your worries. You need to find a way out of this spaceship, and the hallway you dashed down doesn't give you much hope of that. The walls are smooth as glass. There are no seams or handles. No windows to see out of either. Nothing that gives a hint of a door or escape hatch.

So you keep running down what feels like an endless hallway. And that makes you worry. You must be on a larger ship than the one that captured you.

The first opening you come across leads to the right—toward the center of the ship.

To go through the doorway, turn to page 51.
To keep running, turn to page 56.

Once your restraints are loosened, you sit up. The robot reaches out with a clawed hand and grabs your wrist. If you want to escape, it's too late now. You could never pull away from its vise-like grip. Then the robot leads you from the room.

You are led through a short, narrow hallway. You have to duck as you go because the ceiling is so low. Either the aliens are little green men, or this passageway was built for the robots. That makes you wonder, *are there any aliens aboard this ship?*

The robot stops in front of a blank wall. It clicks a couple times. A panel opens to reveal a room. You are pushed through the doorway, and the panel slides shut. You feel around the wall, but you can't find a seam where the door just was.

"It's no use," a familiar voice says behind you.

You turn, surprised to see your friend Jacob. Dozens of people stand behind him looking frightened. They look dirty and ragged compared to the clean, smooth walls surrounding them.

Turn the page

"I've already tried," Jacob says.

"So there's no way out?"

He shakes his head. You verify his answer by looking around the room. There are no other doors, windows, or vents. Just blank walls. You're discouraged, but at least you found your friend.

"I was about a mile from the field when I saw a blue light behind some trees," Jacob says. "I stopped to see what it was, and that's when I saw the UFO. I tried texting you, but it didn't seem like they were going through."

You look around again before asking the question that most worries you, "What do you think they're going to do with us?"

"I have no idea," Jacob says. You're not sure how long you are locked up in the room. It could be minutes or hours. Time seems stuck within the blank walls. Every now and then, another person is pushed through the doorway that suddenly appears and then disappears.

Just when you think the room could hold no one else, a door slides open in the far wall.

Two robots enter the room. They have metal rods that emit a green light. When they wave a rod toward you, you feel nauseous. Using the rods, the aliens force all of you to move.

You exit the spaceship, happy to be on solid ground again. You're forced into a large holding pen with thousands of people. No one seems to know what will happen next or how long you will have to wait here. You simply know that the aliens will eventually leave. You just worry what the planet will be like when they do.

THE END

To follow another path, turn to page 10.
To learn more about aliens, turn to page 101.

You quickly unroll the sleeping bags and clear out some space on the lowest shelf. You have the boys and their babysitter crawl under the shelf. Then you cover them with the sleeping bags.

There is also a Mylar blanket in what looks to be an outdoor survival kit. You pull it over you and hunch down, ducking into the bottom shelf.

All of a sudden, the sick feeling goes away.

Did the aliens leave?

You peak through an opening in the blanket. Everything is still lit up in green light. You look over to the girl and boys. Their sleeping bags are sprawled out on the floor, as if they had passed out. You realize the Mylar blanket must be protecting you.

You hear something bump against the front door upstairs. Then there's the sound of splintering wood.

The floor creaks above you.

To fight back, turn to page 59.
To stay hidden, turn to page 75.

You grab some sleeping bags and hand them to the girl.

"Hide under these," you say.

"What are you going to do?" the girl asks.

"I'm not really sure," you say as you grab the hatchet. "But maybe I can keep them from getting to you and the boys."

Slowly, you creep upstairs. With each step, you feel more and more sick. The effects of the green light are dizzying.

Then you hear the front door burst open. A humming sound enters the farmhouse and moves from room to room. You wait for it to come near the cellar door, trying not to vomit from the UFO's beam.

Then you throw the door open to find a robot. Antennas click and whirl in your direction.

Turn the page

You raise the axe to strike at the robot. But the effects of the green light are overpowering. Your gut wrenches, and you double over. Then your legs give out. You collapse, unconscious.

When you wake, you are strapped to a table. A blinding light shines down on you, forcing you to look away. Your gaze turns to a robot. Its arms end in needles, scalpels, and other terrifying things.

The robot makes two beeping sounds. There's a pause before it makes three more beeps. Then five, then seven.

Are the beeps forming a pattern, like Morse code? Is it trying to communicate? The robot repeats the series of beeps one more time. Two. Three. Five. Seven.

If you know what the beeps mean, turn to page 63.
If you don't know what they mean, turn to page 65.

Going through the doorway seems as good an option as any. It opens into a large circular chamber. You are actually on the second level of the room, on a balcony looking down. Below you are several robots. They scurry about and fiddle with buttons and knobs along the room's walls.

You are amazed by what you see along the walls. The lower level of the room is covered with a bank of clear tubes filled with yellowish liquid. Inside each tube floats an alien. You can't see much of them. A tangle of wires is connected to their bodies, sticking out from their eyes, ears, mouths, and chests.

Turn the page

As you stand there, a buzz fills the air. Then all the robots leave the room.

They know I've escaped. They're looking for me.

Behind you, a panel slides over the doorway—you're now stuck in the room. There are no stairs or ladders to the main level, but the drop is only a few feet. You hang down from the balcony and then let yourself fall.

You quickly glance around to make sure there aren't any robots near. The room is clear, so you walk up to the nearest alien-filled tube. It looks like they are asleep.

This must be how they stay alive during their long journeys through space.

Turn the page

But there is something else. As you examine one of the tubes, you notice that there are several small screens all around it. You touch one of them, and it flickers on.

What you see horrifies you. Several small alien ships hover over a factory. They send down red bolts of light that explode on impact. Chunks of debris fly everywhere as fires blaze. In the background, frightened people scream and run from the destruction.

This must be happening now, you think.

You touch another screen. This one shows the same scene, but from a different angle.

It's the view from a different ship.

You touch another screen, and you get yet another angle of the attack.

As you watch, you notice that the alien in the tube twitches and jerks slightly each time a blast is fired.

Then it dawns on you. You definitely aren't on one of the small scout ships. You are on the mother ship, or at least a command ship. Possibly the larger blue light you saw earlier tonight. And this is the ship's command center. Each of these aliens must be monitoring and directing an attack on Earth.

Thoughts whirl around in your head. *What should I do? What can I do?*

There must be some way to help the people who are being attacked.

As you stand there, unsure what to do next, a door panel slides open behind you. You turn to see a robot enter the room. It's similar to the one that was in the exam room.

When its antennas whip around toward you, it starts to beep and click. Then several metal arms pop out of panels in its body. Each one ends in a menacing clawed hand.

To try to escape, turn to page 68.
To attack the robot, turn to page 69.

You jog down the hallway as fast as you can. As you do, you run your hands along the walls. You hope to feel a seam where a door might be because you can't see any.

You worry that you are just running in a circle. But you haven't passed by the opening where the exam room was.

Suddenly, a door panel opens in front of you. Out pops a robot, only this one isn't like any you've seen so far. It has a more menacing look. It is bullet-shaped with a red glowing top.

An attack robot!

A beam of light bursts from the top of the robot. You duck as the beam shoots past you and scorches the wall.

Zzzzztt!

Turn the page

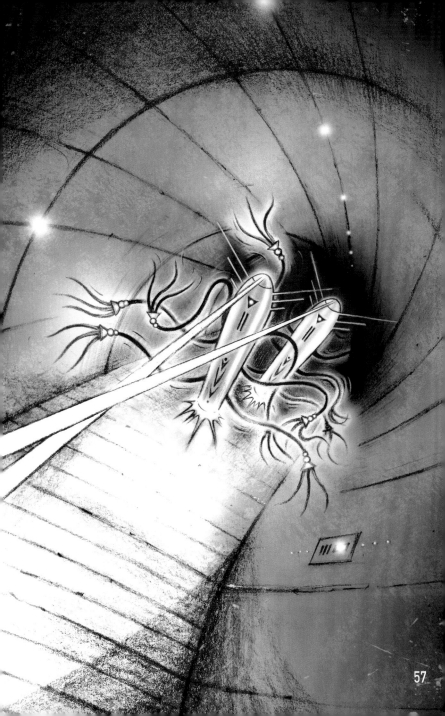

You turn and run back the way you came, hoping to get away. But then another beam of light grazes your shoulder, and you feel a burning pain.

Zzzzztt!

As you run, another panel opens to your right. A metallic hand reaches out and grabs your wrist. It's another one of the attack robots. You duck as it shoots a blast of light at you.

Zzzzztt!

With all your might, you try to pull your hand from its grip, but it's too strong. You're trapped. As you struggle, more robots come at you from both directions.

Zzzzztt!

You avoid the first blast, but the next one hits you in the chest. You slump over as your eyelids close.

THE END

To follow another path, turn to page 10.
To learn more about aliens, turn to page 101.

You hear the door leading to the basement open. Then a humming noise approaches. Peeking through a crease in the Mylar blanket, you see a blue light descending from above. It gets brighter as it gets nearer. They you see a metallic arm reach for the girl. She is dragged from her hiding spot.

You can only hear what happens next. The whirl of the robot's arms. The sleeping bag crumbling to the ground. It must have picked her up. Then the blue light starts to move back upstairs.

You remember seeing the hatchet on the shelf with the rest of the camping gear. In one smooth motion, you stand—keeping the Mylar blanket wrapped around you—and grab the weapon.

Your movement attracts the attention of the robot. Its antennas turn, clicking and whirling in your direction.

Turn the page

But before the robot can act, you swing the hatchet as hard as you can.

Clang!

You put a dent in its top. You swing again and knock off an antenna.

Then arms shoot out from several openings in the robot's body. They end in clawed hands that snap and reach for you.

You hit one with the hatchet as it tears at your shirt. Another reaches for your ankle, but you kick it away. All the while, you keep wildly swinging the axe. You knock off more antennas. Several of the robot's arms are limp and dangling.

You've also suffered several cuts and bruises. But when the robot drops the girl, you know you've won this fight.

The robot quickly retreats up the stairs and disappears through the doorway.

Turn the page

You drag the unconscious girl back to the shelves. You find a couple more Mylar blankets and cover her up. Then you spread blankets over the boys.

You're not sure how, but the Mylar blanket protected you from the aliens' green beam. It seemed to keep the robot from detecting you. So you hope the blankets will keep the girl and boys safe.

Then from upstairs, you hear some loud buzzing. It sounds like more robots have entered the house. You need to get out and either lead the aliens away from the farmhouse or somehow distract them.

You check one of the basement's narrow windows and unhook the latch. It is just wide enough for you to crawl through. You are careful to make sure that you keep the Mylar blanket wrapped around you.

To find the alien craft, turn to page 72.
To make a run for it, turn to page 77.

Prime numbers! you think. *That's what the numbers are.*

You vaguely recall reading somewhere that math is the universal language. Maybe that's how the alien species is trying to communicate with humans.

Upon your recognition, the robot clicks and whirls. Then it unstraps you from the table. A claw hand shoots out and grabs your wrist in a vise-like grip. Any thoughts of escape leave your mind—there's no way you could pull away from the robot now.

The robot leads you down a short, narrow hallway. You have to duck as you go. At the end of the hallway, a door slides open. You are pushed through and enter a large room similar to an arena. It's filled with hundreds, maybe thousands, of people. They all mill about, not sure what to do. You wonder if you know any of them.

Turn the page

A hand reaches out of the crowd and grabs your shoulder. You spin around. It's Jacob!

"Jacob! What happened to you?" you ask.

"I got zapped by one of their green lights and ended up here," he replies. "You?"

"Same," you say. "So what do they want?" You nod your head toward a bullet-shaped robot that is patrolling outside the pen.

"Food. At least, that's the rumor," Jacob says.

"They're going to eat us?" you ask worriedly.

"No," Jacob says. "Anyone who passes their intelligence test is safe as long as they don't fight back."

So like the rest of the imprisoned people, you wait. You wait for the aliens to take what they want from your planet. There is nothing else you can do, but you hope that Earth will be able to sustain the human race after the aliens leave.

THE END

To follow another path, turn to page 10.
To learn more about aliens, turn to page 101.

The alien robot pushes a button. All of a sudden, green light washes over you. You feel sick, like you're going to throw up or pass out. You kick and struggle against your restraints, but it's no use. Nausea overwhelms you, and you black out.

You wake to the sound of mooing.

Is that a cow? you wonder.

Then you hear the grunt of a pig and the bleat of a sheep. For a brief moment, you think you're on a farm or in a dimly lit barn. But then the memories rush back at you. You remember the UFO, the robots, and the green beam of light that knocked you out.

You sit up and see that you are in a large room. You can barely see the distant walls in the dim light. Cows, pigs, and other farm animals roam freely about.

"He's awake," a voice says to your right.

You turn to see a group of people huddled together. You get up and walk over to them.

"Where are we?" you ask.

Turn the page

A sad-looking man turns to you and says, "The food pens, we think."

"What?" you ask, horrified.

"Yeah," a woman adds. "We think the aliens invaded Earth to gather food."

In a way, that makes sense to you. Earth has metals and ores, but the aliens probably have plenty. But every living thing needs food and water to survive, and Earth has plenty of both.

"We think the robot was giving some sort of intelligence test," the man says. "I've seen them apply it to cats and squirrels. Anyone or anything that doesn't pass ends up here."

"So we're gonna be food?" you ask, defeated.

The people just look at each other sadly and then hang their heads. Suddenly, the floor drops out from you, and you fall into darkness.

THE END
To follow another path, turn to page 10.
To learn more about aliens, turn to page 101.

You don't have any weapons. Your only option is to escape. As the robot lunges for you with its clinking hands, you dodge out of the way. Then you dart past it and head for the doorway.

But another robot fills the doorway before you can squeeze through. It reaches out with its metal hands and snags your shirt. You hear a ripping sound as you pull away. Then more clawed hands reach out for your wrist, your thigh, your arm. There are too many too avoid. You're caught. As the robot's grip tightens, you scream in pain.

Then the other robot comes up behind you. Its claws dig into your side and neck. You continue to struggle, but you are helpless to defend yourself as a third robot attacks.

THE END

To follow another path, turn to page 10.
To learn more about aliens, turn to page 101.

The world is being devastated by aliens. But there must be something you can do. You're in one of their command ships. This is probably your best chance to stop them.

As the robot reaches for you, you duck under its grasp and dart around it. Then you push it hard into the wall of screens. Sparks fly, and the robot jerks uncontrollably. Energy courses through its body as one of its arms gets caught in some wiring.

The screen near you flickers and fizzles. You must have shorted some of them out. You wonder if that means the aliens can't see or control the spaceships that the screens are connected to.

Then you feel the ship shudder. You glance at the nearest alien. It's writhing painfully in its tube.

Maybe the aliens in the tubes are in control of this ship too, you think. *And maybe you can hurt them somehow.*

Turn the page

You have an idea. As another robot enters the room, you duck under its grasping arms. You shove it at one of the aliens in a tube.

To your surprise, the tube isn't made of glass or hard plastic—it's a clear, flexible material. As the robot rams into the tube, its outer surface bends inward. That's not what you were expecting. You had hoped the tube would shatter, spilling its contents on the floor.

But then the sharp edges of one of the robot's arms easily cuts through the tube. Yellow fluid starts leaking onto the floor. The alien shakes violently.

Alarms blare. Lights flash. More robots enter the room. But before they can attack you, the ship lurches. You and the robots crash into the wall. You feel a thunk on the back of your head, and everything goes black.

Turn to page 90.

As soon as you're through the window, you duck behind a shrub. Looking up, you can't see the alien ship. You think it may have landed in front of the house.

With your hatchet and Mylar blanket, you creep toward the corner of the house to peek around to the front yard. There the UFO hovers a few yards off the ground. The robot you attacked is below the ship. Some of its arms and broken antennas are still dangling at its side. The robot is beeping and clicking loudly. *Probably communicating with the ship*, you think.

Then two bullet-shaped robots come out of the house to join the banged-up robot. It doesn't look like they've found the girl and boys.

Suddenly, the green beam of light shuts off, and the robots go silent. A hatch opens in the bottom of the ship. A figure descends from the hatch, floating on a blue metal disc. It's covered in a metallic suit and wearing a helmet. Slung over its back is a weapon.

A ray gun!

Turn the page

The alien floats over to the damaged robot and looks it over. Then the alien glances at the two bullet-shaped robots, which have started to click and beep again.

The alien motions toward the front door. One of the robots darts through it as the alien follows. The other robot stations itself outside.

To protect the girl and boys, turn to page 81.

To capture the alien ship, turn to page 86.

You tuck the Mylar blanket tightly around you. Then you lean back under the shelving as far as you can.

The creaking upstairs moves throughout the house, then to the stairs leading down to the basement. You hear a humming noise approach. As it gets louder, a blue light fills the basement. You can see its glow through the blanket.

Then you hear some ruffling near you. It sounds as if the girl and boys are being dragged from their hiding spots. But you don't dare move. You could get caught too, or worse.

After a few moments, you hear the basement steps creak. Then the blue light begins to fade.

When all is finally quiet in the house, you unwrap yourself from the blanket.

Turn the page

Next to you, the shelves are empty. The boys and girl are gone. They have been taken by the aliens.

To your surprise, the Mylar blanket not only protected you from the alien's green beam, but it also must have kept you from being detected. You doubt the aliens even knew you were there.

You feel guilty about letting the girl and boys get captured. But what could you have done?

Aliens have invaded the planet, and Earth's armies are destroyed. But in the coming days and weeks, what you've discovered about the Mylar blankets will prove to be important. After the initial attack, people begin to fight back, including you. And you could never have helped if you had been captured. You just hope what you've learned is enough to survive the invasion.

THE END

To follow another path, turn to page 10.
To learn more about aliens, turn to page 101.

The alien ship has landed in front of the house, so you duck around back and head into the woods. You take cover behind some nearby trees and then run until you are out of breath.

You're not sure how far you make it before collapsing to the ground, exhausted. You are tired and afraid. You don't know what to do next.

As you sit there, you hear the crunch of approaching footsteps. You jump to your feet, ready to flee. But instead of a robot, you see a person walk out from behind a tree. Then another. In all there are six people slowly creeping through the woods in your direction.

"Hey!" you shout.

They all stop.

"Keep it down," one of the people snaps.

Turn the page

Once the group has gathered around you, one of them asks, "Where did you come from?"

"And what's that you're wearing?" another man adds, pointing to the Mylar blanket. You tell them about first spotting the UFO and fleeing. Then you explain about the farmhouse and hiding from the aliens.

"You say that blanket protected you from the UFO's green beam?" one asks.

"Yeah, and there's more in the farmhouse," you say. "But there's an alien ship there."

"A small one or a big one?" the man asks.

"I don't know," you say. "It's about 20 feet across."

"That's a small one," a woman says.

"It's not a command ship then," the man answers.

"Yeah, those usually don't get too close to the surface," another person adds.

"So probably just a scout ship with a couple attack robots," the man says. "We can take it." The people around him nod in agreement.

Turn the page

You're surprised at their confidence, but as you look closer at the group, you notice that many of the people have weapons. Rifles are strapped over their backs, and pistols are holstered on their sides.

"We've just started setting up a resistance in this area," the man explains. "Will you join us?"

You think back to the girl and the boys in the farmhouse. You feel bad for leaving them there, and this will be an opportunity to see if they're safe.

"Yes," you say.

You join one of many small guerrilla groups that are fighting back against the aliens. You're told it could be a long fight, but the longer you survive, the better your odds are of defeating the aliens.

THE END

To follow another path, turn to page 10.
To learn more about aliens, turn to page 101.

The girl and the boys are still in the basement. You worry that they could be in danger with the alien in the house.

The front door is guarded by a robot, so you head back to the window. You crawl through it. You go over to the girl and boys. Now that the green light is off, they are stirring and starting to wake.

"Shhh," you say and point upstairs.

As if on cue, the floor creaks. The girl nods and pulls the boys to her.

With the hatchet poised to strike, you hide behind the stairs. Then the door swings open. You hear the stairs creak. You see a metallic boot on the step above you. The alien slowly descends.

Turn the page

You strike when you see the back of the alien's helmeted head. The axe cracks open the helmet. You get a whiff of foul-smelling air. The alien collapses to the ground, coughing and hacking, as if Earth's air is toxic to it.

You kick the alien over and take its weapon. Instead of a trigger, there's a place to put your hand in. When you grab it, the weapon wraps around your hand like a glove, as if it's now part of you.

From up the stairs, you hear clicking. You turn to see one of the attack robots at the top of the stairs. Its head is glowing bright red. You aim the weapon, but you don't know how to fire it.

I need to shoot, you think. As you think it, it happens. The ray gun fires, blasting a hole in the attack robot. From outside, you hear buzzing and beeping. The other robot appears at the top of the stairs, and you blast it too.

Turn the page

Once you're sure that the danger is over, you turn to the alien. It lays lifeless on the floor. You're surprised that in many ways, its face looks human, but with grayer skin and large black eyes. It has eyebrows, a nose, and a pair of thin lips.

You motion to the girl to follow you. Then you creep up the stairs. There are no other aliens or robots around. You only wish you could call someone to tell them what you did, what you've found. That there's an alien spacecraft sitting outside.

That's when you see it. A phone mounted to a wall.

"You still have a land line?" you ask the girl.

She nods. "Reception is bad out here."

You pick up the phone and dial 9-1-1.

"9-1-1, what's your emergency?"

"I just killed an alien!" you blurt out excitedly. You quickly retell your story.

"A team is on its way," the voice says, and then hangs up. Apparently, you're not the first person to call in about the alien invasion.

You turn to the girl, "Help is coming."

You realize that defeating the aliens will be a long fight. But you have a weapon that will add some firepower to your side.

THE END

To follow another path, turn to page 10.
To learn more about aliens, turn to page 101.

You are not sure which way the robot is facing—or if it even has a face. To play it safe, you pick up a rock and toss it to the far side of the yard, away from the ship. When it hits the ground, the robot's antennas go wild and whirl in the direction of the rock. The top of the robot starts to glow red with energy.

You pick up another rock and throw it farther and off to the side. The robot quickly heads in that direction. Then you make a dash for the spaceship.

The hatch on the bottom is still open, but there's no ladder. You leap up and grab ahold of the rim of the hatch. As your feet kick wildly below, you feel a hot blast shoot past.

The robot's seen me!

You grunt and quickly pull yourself up into the ship just as another blast shoots past you.

You crawl up inside the ship. The space you find yourself in isn't large, possibly 6 feet in diameter and only a few feet high. It has a circular shape, with lights and panels covering the entire wall. In the center is a chair.

Just then, you hear a buzzing sound from below. You glance through the hatch to see the attack robot. Its antennas are aimed in your direction. The top starts to glow red as you duck back into the ship's cockpit.

There's no escape now, so you only have one choice. You sit down in the chair.

What happens next both frightens and amazes you. Wires and tubes spring out of panels from the wall. Some wires imbed themselves into the tips of your fingers while tubes latch onto your eyes.

Turn the page

Suddenly, instead of seeing what's around you, you're sensing what's around the ship. You hear the rustling of leaves. You feel the breeze flowing around you and even smell the aromas in the night air. You're so amazed by it all that you almost forget where you are and what's happening.

Then the attack robot below the ship buzzes, catching your attention. It's signaling to the alien and other attack robot as they rush out of the house. The alien raises its weapon.

I have to defend myself, you think.

As the thought passes through your head, an energy field rises up around the ship. The field deflects the blast from the alien's weapon.

To attack the alien, turn to page 94.
To fly off, turn to page 96.

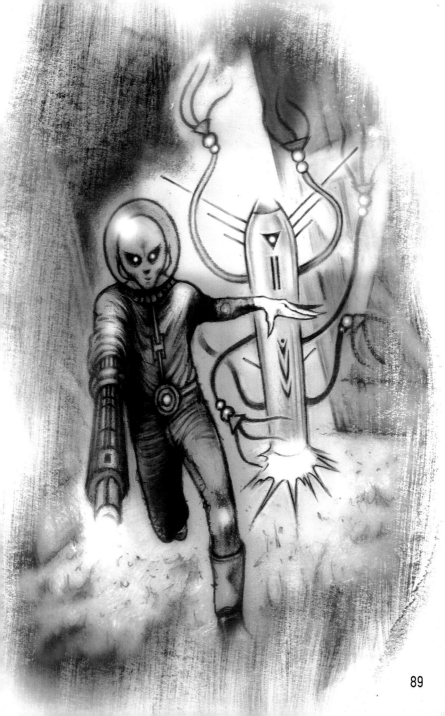

When you come to, your world is filled with smoke and sparks. You see a flashing screen and broken tubes. You try to stand, but you can't keep your balance. The floor is tilted at a drastic angle. The ship has crashed into Earth's surface!

All around you lies destruction. Yellow fluid is leaking out of tubes. Alien bodies are sprawled on the floor. Some are dead. Others are gasping and coughing. You wonder if Earth's air is toxic to them.

You manage to untangle yourself from the wreckage. Then you crawl through the room's twisted doorway. You search the ship until you find an open hatch that leads out. As you crawl through it, a hand reaches for you from outside the ship and pulls you out.

Turn the page

As you're dragged from the wreckage, a voice asks, "How'd you survive that crash?" You are pulled to your feet by a heavily armed man wearing camouflage fatigues.

"I dunno," you say as you shrug your shoulders. "Luck, I guess."

"Come on, we need to get out of here," the man says. "They might come see what happened to their command ship."

Debris is everywhere. Big chunks of metal cover the ground. The man leads you out of the wreckage and toward a cluster of trees. There a ragtag group of men and women are waiting. They are all armed and look at you with suspicion.

"Where did he come from?" a woman asks.

"I was inside the ship," you say. The man with you nods, as if to confirm your story. "I was fighting with some robots in its command center when all this happened." You motion back toward the wreckage.

"You brought down a command ship?" a man asks, shocked.

"I've seen an F22 unload everything it had on one of those and not leave a scratch," another says.

You see the suspicion in the soldiers' eyes turn to respect. Pride wells up in your chest.

"We need to tell the others what you found inside," says the man who helped you out of the wreckage.

You soon learn that these men and women are all part of an organized resistance. The next days and weeks are dangerous. You're constantly running and hiding from the aliens. But so far, you are believed to be the only person who has seen what's inside an alien ship and escaped to tell about it.

The information you have is crucial to the resistance. The soldiers you meet and talk to believe it will help defeat the aliens.

THE END
To follow another path, turn to page 10.
To learn more about aliens, turn to page 101.

The next thought that goes through your head is that you should attack. From the bottom of the ship, a red bolt of energy shoots forward. It disintegrates the alien and attack robot next to it.

I did that by just thinking it, you marvel.

You see the other attack robot fleeing toward some trees. You think of shooting it. Another energy bolt shoots from the spaceship and destroys the robot.

Cool!

With the alien dead and the attack robots destroyed, you think of escaping. The spaceship lurches, almost if it doesn't know where to go. You think "up," and it rises up. You're quickly hundreds of feet in the air. Even high off the ground, you can still sense everything around the ship. You see stars twinkling overhead.

Then you think "forward," and the ship races forward.

You are amazed at how easy it is to fly the spaceship, but you also wonder how you will disengage from all the wires and tubes connected to you.

In your mind, you keep hearing a series of clicks and whistles. You're not sure what they mean. You wish you could put your finger in your ear to stop the noise, but tubes cover them, and wires entangle your fingers.

Suddenly, the ship shudders, like it was hit by something.

Am I under attack?

Your senses pick up an approaching ship. It's not a small scout ship like the one you're in. It's an attack ship. It fires, and a wave of energy crackles over your ship. Your shields are knocked out.

Before you can think to flee, the attack ship fires again. Your ship explodes in a fiery ball.

THE END
To follow another path, turn to page 10.
To learn more about aliens, turn to page 101.

You are amazed that you have control of the alien ship and how easy it is to fly. You just think "up," and it shoots upward. It's easier than using a video game controller.

The ship is only a small one, but you think it could definitely be useful. You could learn about the aliens' technology and maybe even find a way to fight back against the invaders. You just need to get it away from here, before more aliens come.

As if it's reading your mind, the ship lurches forward a few feet.

Why won't it go?

You realize you need to think where you want it to go. In the distance, you see a thick grove of trees.

I can hide the ship in there.

As you think it, the ship zooms forward.

Turn the page

While you are flying, you hear some clicking and buzzing in your brain. There's a pattern to it, almost as if it were speech. You worry that the aliens are trying to communicate with the ship.

What will they do if they realize a human is flying it? you wonder.

Once you reach the trees, you set the ship down. You doubt you will be safe here for long, but you need a moment to figure out what to do. Then you think about the ship powering down. Suddenly, the wires and tubes retract. You hope that shutting down the ship will prevent the aliens from tracking it.

You exit through the hatch and jump out. You're surprised to see several armed people surrounding you.

"Hey, he's not an alien," a woman says.

A man pokes you in the arm. "You human?"

"Yes! Don't shoot!" you shout, raising your hands in the air.

"Then you better explain how you picked up this ride," the man says.

You quickly retell your story, starting with first spotting the UFO and ending with the Mylar blankets and escaping with the ship. When you finish, the man in charge of the group tells you that they are setting up a resistance in this area. They are so impressed by your actions that they ask you to join them.

While it will be a long fight to rid Earth of the invaders, you have a good start. You have one of their ships. Maybe you can learn something about their technology that will help you fight back.

THE END

To follow another path, turn to page 10.
To learn more about aliens, turn to page 101.

LIFE AMONG THE STARS

Today scientists are able to locate planets among the hundreds of billions of stars in our galaxy, the Milky Way. They can even estimate which planets are similar in size, possess water, and circle a star similar to Earth's sun.

It is believed that billions of planets could be orbiting stars in what is known as the Goldilocks' zone. This area is close enough to a star to be warm but not too far away to be overly cold. This zone is believed to be perfect for the possibility of life. But because of their distance from Earth, we cannot determine whether life actually exists on any of these planets. However, that doesn't stop people from speculating that aliens have ventured to Earth.

Some people believe aliens have been visiting our planet for thousands of years. Some even think that alien technology helped build ancient marvels, from the pyramids to the giant statues on Easter Island.

People simply find it difficult to imagine that ancient civilizations had the ability to build these structures, so they credit aliens. But most of these theories have been debunked. Large sleds have been found in Egypt that were used to move the massive rocks that formed the pyramids. The statues on Easter Island are thought to have been brought there by boat—not alien ships.

The speculation that aliens have visited Earth often focuses on UFO sightings. Perhaps the most famous of them occurred in Roswell, New Mexico. In July 1947, a rancher named William Brazel reported finding debris from a flying saucer. An officer from the local air base went to investigate. A few days later, a headline in the *Roswell Daily Record* read "RAAF Captures Flying Saucer on Ranch in Roswell Region." The military quickly denied this, stating that what was found was actually a weather balloon. But many wild tales sprung up about the events at Roswell. Some people even claim they saw alien bodies being recovered from the wreckage.

While reports of alien encounters can sound exciting, stories of alien abductions have terrified people. One of the first reported abductions involved Barney and Betty Hill of New Hampshire. On a night in September 1961, the couple was driving home when they saw what they claimed to be a UFO. Sometime later, the Hills discovered that their drive home took two hours longer than it should have—they were missing two hours of time.

Through hypnosis, the Hills recounted being stopped by the aliens. They said they were taken aboard the alien craft and given medical examinations. But so far, alien abductions have been as difficult to prove as alien encounters. The only evidence comes from eyewitness accounts.

It's not hard to imagine the possibility of alien life somewhere among the stars. The universe is virtually limitless, so it's possible that there is life out there somewhere.

But none of the stories about alien encounters or abductions answer one key question: Why would aliens visit Earth? If you ask scientists, such as Stephen Hawking, it might be for conquest. Why else would they risk traveling billions of miles through space?

Just don't expect the aliens to be little green men. We send robots to explore distant planets. Aliens could do the same. The trip from their planet to ours might be too long and pose too many dangers for living creatures to survive.

We may never know if the stories about alien encounters and abductions hold any truth. Still, it's exciting to look up at the stars and imagine what extraterrestrial beings might live beyond our own solar system. And if so, what the intent of their trip could be.

ALIEN INVASION
SURVIVAL GUIDE

The key thing to remember is that alien technology would probably be more advanced than ours. If their ships can travel billions of miles through space, their weapons will be far more destructive as well.

But there is still hope. You just need to survive the initial onslaught. You'll need a survival kit that will help you in any situation:

SURVIVAL KIT

*Flint stone for making fire (waterproof matches will work also, but you may run out of them)

*Iodine tablets for making water drinkable

*Utility knife

*First aid kit

*Fishing kit, with line, hooks, and sinkers

*Nylon rope, at least 25 feet

*Compass and map of area where you live

*Tarp, to use for shelter

*Whistle, to use as an alarm in case of danger

*Mylar blanket, for warmth

*Poncho, gloves, and stocking cap

*Duct tape, for repairs

*Plastic bags, for storage

*Wire, at least 25 feet

*Cooking pots and eating utensils

*Hand-crank radio

*Flashlights, with spare batteries

*Walkie-talkies, with spare batteries

*Jacket, hiking shoes, and an extra pair of warm clothes

*Stainless steel water bottle

*Bottled water (as much as you can carry)

*Nonperishable food (snack bars, jerky, instant soup, and cereal)

TOP 10 SURVIVAL TIPS FOR AN ALIEN INVASION

- Any weapons you find probably won't match what the aliens possess. Your best defense is to hide.

- Get as far away from the alien forces as possible. Consider using underground tunnels and remote wilderness areas to hide in.

- Avoid populated areas. Large groups of people could attract the invaders' attention. There will also be more competition for resources, such as food and water, where masses of people gather.

- Avoid factories and military bases. These will likely be the first places that aliens attack in order to disable our ability to fight back.

- Avoid traveling on major roadways. They will likely be blocked with traffic and debris.

- Make sure your hiding places have multiple escape routes. Your first plan of escape might be blocked, so it's best to have more than one way to run from danger.

- It will be easier to survive in small groups than alone. Keep your friends and family with you. You will be able to work together to find food, keep watch for each other, and help one another should someone get hurt.

- Remember the three key things that you need to survive: shelter, food, and water. Anything you bring with you must help obtain one of these essentials.

- You might not see any actual aliens during an alien invasion. If aliens attack, they might send robots because it would be difficult to survive the long trip to our planet. So don't just be on the lookout for little green creatures.

- The longer you survive, the better chance the aliens will be defeated. Someone will either find a weakness in the aliens' technology or start a resistance to fight back against the invaders. The longer people can resist, the less likely the aliens will be willing to stay and fight, using up resources they need to return home.

GLOSSARY

ABDUCTION (ab-DUK-shun)—the act of kidnapping, or taking someone against his or her will

ASTRONOMY (uh-STRAH-nuh-mee)—the study of stars, planets, and other objects in space

DEBUNK (dee-BUNK)—to disprove something

EXTRATERRESTRIAL (ek-struh-tuh-RESS-tree-uhl)—a life form that comes from outer space; extraterrestrial means "outside of Earth"

GUERRILLA (guh-RIL-ah)—warfare using small, surprise attacks rather than large battles

METEOR (MEE-tee-ur)—a piece of rock or dust that enters the earth's atmosphere, causing a streak of light in the sky

NAUSEA (NAW-zee-uh)—a feeling of sickness in the stomach that may cause vomiting

SATELLITE (SAT-uh-lite)—a spacecraft used to send signals and information from one place to another

SPECULATION (speh-kyoo-LAY-shuhn)—ideas or guesses about something that is unknown

READ MORE

Hile, Lori. *Aliens and UFOs.* Chicago: Raintree, 2014.

Kincade, Chris. *Encountering Aliens: Eyewitness Accounts.* North Mankato, Minn.: Capstone Press, 2015.

Marden, Kathleen, and Denise Stoner. *Making Contact: Alien Abduction Case Studies.* New York: Rosen Publishing, 2015.

Rivkin, Jennifer. *Searching for UFOs.* New York: PowerKids Press, 2015.

INTERNET SITES

Use FactHound to find Internet sites related to this book. All of the sites on FactHound have been researched by our staff.

Here's all you do:
Visit *www.facthound.com*
Type in this code: 9781491458532

AUTHOR

Blake Hoena wrote his first story in second grade. It was about space aliens trying to steal the moon. And ever since, he has been fascinated with little green men. He even created a graphic novel series about alien brothers, Eek and Ack, who try to conquer our big blue home. When not thinking about outer space, Blake writes children's books about mythology, skateboarding, and poetry. He lives in St. Paul, Minnesota, with his wife, two kids, and a couple of pets.

ILLUSTRATOR

Paul Fisher-Johnson graduated with a degree in Illustration from Swindon College's School of Art and Design. His work has been published more than 70 times and includes book covers, internal illustration, and even corporate greeting cards. Paul illustrates in both color and black and white, with a special strength for figurative work. He currently lives near Bristol, England, with his three children and spends his spare time writing music to perform with his band.